Why do people get ill?

FOX EYE
PUBLISHING

Why do people get ill?

People get ill when their bodies are not able to work properly.

Why are they not able to work properly?

Sometimes it is because a part of us has become faulty.

Sometimes it is because tiny, invisible things called germs are attacking our insides.

Our bodies can fight off germs with something already inside us called an immune system.

but some germs can be very strong, and we may need extra help to stop the germs attacking us.

That is why we may visit a Doctor, or a Nurse or go to a hospital.

Doctors and Nurses will know what type of extra help is needed, and hospitals have the special machines to help us get well again.

Why do we get germs inside us?

Germs are in the air we breathe in, and on anything that's not very clean.

So doing things like washing our hands before we eat can stop germs getting inside us.

Let's find out about the ways we can stay well.

Turn the page over to discover the answers to these questions.

Why must we eat lots of different foods?
Why should we not overeat?
Why must I wash myself every day?
Why must I tell someone if I'm not feeling well?

Let's find out about staying safe.

The answers are ...

Eating lots of different foods helps us get enough of all the minerals and vitamins our body needs.
Eating too much can make us too big and heavy, which makes it harder for our body parts to work properly and can make them go weak.
Keeping the outside of your body clean can help to stop germs getting inside you and making you ill.
If other people know you are ill they can help you to get better quicker.

How to use this book

You can read this book with one child or a group of children.

The book can be used to begin a discussion around complex questions such as learning why we get ill.

The book is also a reading aid, with enlarged and repeated words to help children to develop their reading skills.

How to read the story

Before beginning the story, ensure that the children you are reading to are relaxed and focused.

Take time to look at the enlarged words and the illustrations, and discuss what this book might be about before reading the story.

New words can be tricky for young children to approach.

Sounding them out first, slowly and repeatedly, can help children to learn the words and become familiar with them.

Did you spot
the Tardigrade
hiding in
this book?

First published in 2023 by Fox Eye Publishing
Unit 31, Vulcan House Business Centre,
Vulcan Road, Leicester, LE5 3EF
www.foxeyepublishing.com

Written and illustrated by Simon Couchman

ISBN 978-1-80445-357-5

A catalogue record for this book is available from the British Library.

Printed in China

Titles in the Series

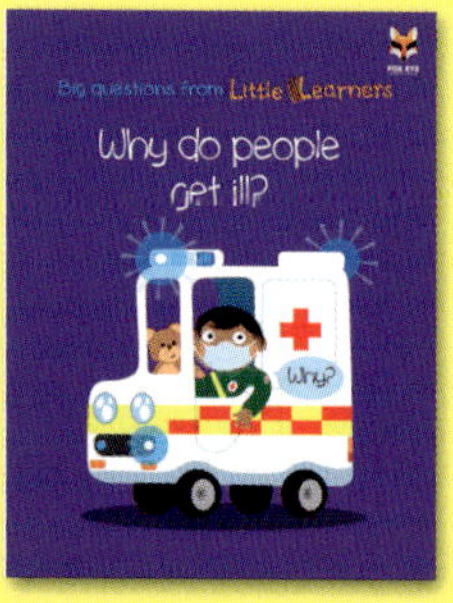

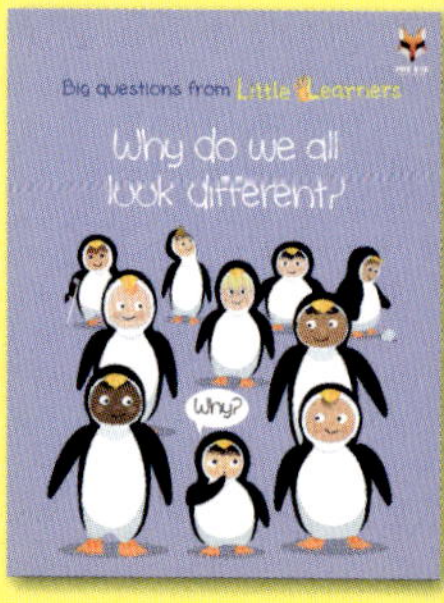

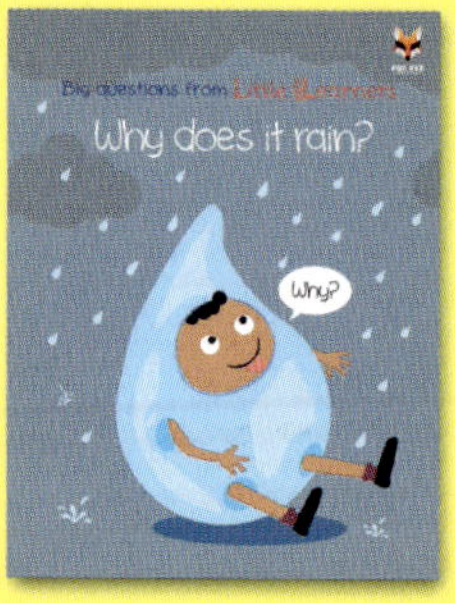

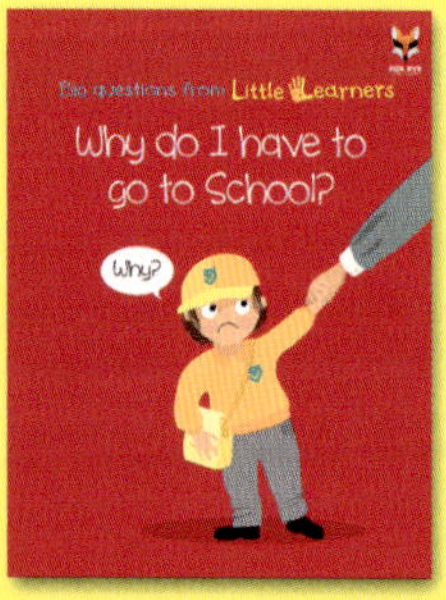

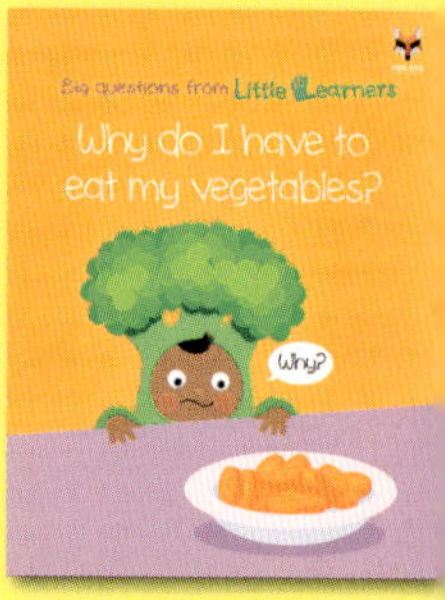